Molly and Polly

by Sharon Fear • illustrated by Marsha Serafin

MODERN CURRICULUM PRESS
Pearson Learning Group

Can you say bell?
Can you?

Bell! Bell! Bell!
Polly

Can you say cracker?
Can you?
Molly

Cracker.
Cracker, cracker!
Polly

Yes!
You did it!

Yes.
Yes, yes!

Bell! Bell! Bell!

What did he say?
What?

Dad!
Our dog cannot say that!

Cracker!
Cracker, cracker!

Dad!
Our dog cannot say that!

Come on.
Tell us.
Did you say that?

Did you say that?
Did you?
Molly

Yes, yes, yes!
Polly